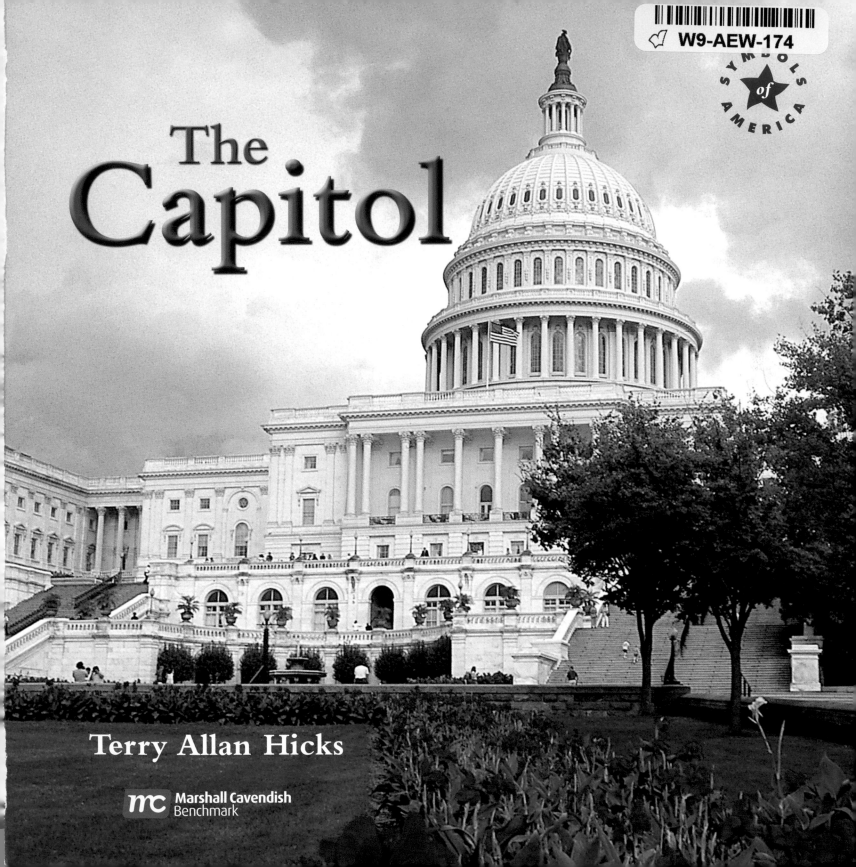

SYMBOLS of AMERICA

The Capitol

Terry Allan Hicks

mc **Marshall Cavendish**
Benchmark

Marshall Cavendish
99 White Plains Road
Tarrytown, New York 10591-9001
www.marshallcavendish.us

All Web sites were available and accurate when this book was sent to press.

Library of Congress Cataloging-in-Publication Data
Hicks, Terry Allan.
The Capitol / by Terry Allan Hicks.
p. cm. — (Symbols of America)
Summary: "An exploration of the construction and history of this important government
building in Washington, D.C., that has become an American symbol"—Provided by publisher.
Includes bibliographical references (p. 38) and index.
ISBN 978-0-7614-3374-3 (PB)
ISBN 978-0-7614-2132-0 (HB)
1. United States Capitol (Washington, D.C.)—Juvenile literature. 2. Washington (D.C.)
—Buildings, structures, etc.—Juvenile literature.
I. Title. II. Series: Hicks, Terry Allan. Symbols of America.

F204.C2H53 2006
975.3—dc22
2005020607

Photo research by Anne Burns Images

Front cover photo: ACESTOCK.com
Back cover photo: U.S. Postal Service

The photographs in this book are used by permission and through the courtesy of: *ACESTOCK.com*: 1, 4. *SuperStock:* Brian
Lawrence, 7; Robert Llewellyn, 35. *Jay Mallin:* 8, 24, 28. *Corbis:* Alan Schein, 11; Corbis, 19, 23; Joseph Shom/Visions of
America, 27; Kelly-Mooney Photography, 31; Richard T. Nowitz, 32. *North Wind Picture Archives:* 12, 19 (inset), 20. *The
Granger Collection:* 15, 16.

Series design by Adam Mietlowski

Printed in Malaysia

1 3 5 6 4 2

Contents

CHAPTER ONE

Where Democracy Lives

The city of Washington, D.C., is known for its many grand buildings. One of the greatest of them all is the United States *Capitol*.

The Capitol looks down on Washington, D.C., from the city's highest point. Capitol Hill is 88 feet (27 meters) above the level of the Potomac River. The building itself is more than 288 feet (88 meters) high and 750 feet (229 meters) long. This symbol of America was designed to be the *centerpiece* of the nation's *capital*.

◀ *The Capitol steps, where newly elected presidents are sworn in.*

The city's main streets spread out from Capitol Hill, like the spokes of a huge wheel. The Capitol's dome, with its statue on top, can be viewed from most of the city. It can even be seen from as far away as the state of Virginia.

A visitor standing on the Capitol steps is met with an amazing view. The Washington Monument, the Lincoln Memorial, the Potomac River, and the tree-lined lawns of the National Mall are just a few of the sights that can be seen. The area is especially beautiful at night, when the city's monuments are bathed in light.

The Washington Monument by night, with the Capitol dome in the background. ▶

As grand as the building and its grounds are, it is what goes on inside the Capitol that makes it so important.

The Capitol is the home of the United States *Congress*, the *legislative branch* of the *federal government*. It is here that the men and women who are elected to the *Senate* and the *House of Representatives* write new laws, set taxes, and decide whether or not the United States will go to war.

Did You Know?

Every four years, an important event takes place on the Capitol steps. The newly elected president takes the oath of office there, before walking or riding down Pennsylvania Avenue to begin living in the White House.

◄ *The House of Representatives has met in the Capitol every year since 1807.*

The Capitol is the work of many people. Architects and engineers, statesmen and soldiers, artists and laborers have all helped to make the building what it is today. Through the years, the Capitol has changed many times. It has been built and rebuilt, nearly destroyed by a foreign army, then rebuilt again. But one thing has always stayed the same: The Capitol is still the place where American *democracy* lives.

Members of the United States Coast Guard stand at attention in front of the Capitol. ▶

CHAPTER TWO

Building the Capitol

In 1791 Congress chose to locate the new capital of the United States along the Potomac River. At the time, the area held little more than a few villages and farms. So there was a lot of work to be done. The young government needed many new buildings where its leaders could meet and work.

George Washington, the first president of the United States, helped to choose the place where the Capitol would be built. He and Pierre Charles L'Enfant, the architect and engineer who planned the entire city, walked across the area. L'Enfant discussed with Washington where the city's great buildings should be placed. L'Enfant selected Jenkins Hill, now known as Capitol Hill, as the site of the Capitol.

◀ *Washington, D.C., in 1800—looking nothing like the great city we know today.*

Many architects sent in plans for the Capitol. They were hoping to be the lucky one chosen to build the country's most important building. The winning design came from William Thornton, a doctor who was also an *amateur* architect. Thornton's plan called for two wings. The north wing was for the Senate, and the south for the House of Representatives. These two sections were joined by a great domed central area, called the Rotunda. President Washington was pleased with the plan and approved the design. He laid the building's *cornerstone* on September 18, 1793.

George Washington (left), the nation's first president, lays the cornerstone for the Capitol. ▶

The project began very slowly. The first two architects, Stephen H. Hallet and George Hadfield, were fired for changing the design. There were other problems, too. Many laborers refused to work in an area they sometimes called "a sea of mud." The heavy Virginia sandstone used in the building was hard to haul to the site on river barges. And money was always hard to find.

A new architect, James Hoban, finally got the project moving faster. Because he had designed the White House, he was familiar with building in Washington, D.C. Even so, by the time the government moved to the city, in late 1800, only the Senate's north wing was ready.

◄ *The partially completed Capitol, shown in a print from 1800.*

The project continued under Benjamin Latrobe, who was named the Capitol's architect in 1803. The House of Representatives moved into the south wing in 1807. But there was still work to be done. The project slowed with the start of the War of 1812, a time when the Capitol was nearly destroyed before it was even finished.

The War of 1812, fought between the United States and Great Britain, was hard on Washington, D.C. As the war neared its end, British soldiers *occupied* the city. On August 24, 1814, they set fire to the Capitol, the White House, and several other important buildings. Only a sudden rainstorm kept the Capitol from being burned to the ground.

This blueprint shows the north wing of the Capitol in 1814.
Inset: Benjamin Latrobe is thought to have been the first professional architect in the United States.

▶

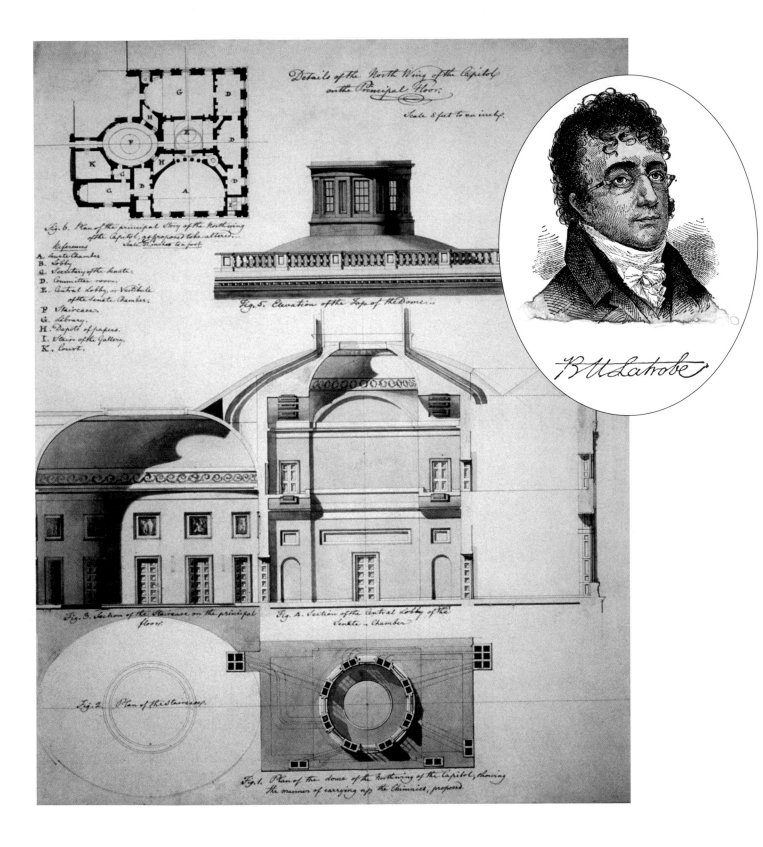

Details of the North Wing of the Capitol on the Principal Floor.

Scale 5 feet to an inch.

Fig. 6. Plan of the principal Story of the North wing of the Capitol, as proposed to be altered. Scale 10 inches to a foot.

References
A. Senate Chamber.
B. Lobby.
C. Secretary of the Senate.
D. Committee room.
E. Central Lobby, or Vestibule of the Senate Chamber.
F. Staircase.
G. Library.
H. Depots of papers.
I. Stairs of the Gallery.
K. Court.

Fig. 5. Elevation of the Top of the Dome.

Fig. 3. Section of the Staircase on the principal floor.

Fig. 4. Section of the Central Lobby of the Senate Chamber.

Fig. 2. Plan of the Staircases.

Fig. 1. Plan of the dome of the North wing of the Capitol, shewing the manner of carrying up the Chimnies, proposed.

B H Latrobe

When the war ended, Benjamin Latrobe began rebuilding the badly damaged Capitol. For the repairs, he chose white Virginia marble. Then, in 1817, he quit the project. A year later, Charles Bulfinch, a well-known architect from Boston, took over. He finished building the most important parts of the Capitol—the House and Senate chambers and the Supreme Court offices. They were ready for use in 1819. Bulfinch also completed the Rotunda, with a domed roof made of wood covered with copper. By 1827, the Capitol was almost done.

◀ *Charles Bulfinch designed many buildings in his native Massachusetts, including the statehouse.*

The young nation was growing quickly. Many new states sent their *representatives* to Washington, D.C. The Capitol was no longer big enough to hold them all. In 1851 Thomas U. Walter, a Philadelphia architect, was given the task of making the building larger.

Walter used more marble, replacing the original sandstone, which was aging badly. He also removed the original wooden dome, which was too small and a fire hazard as well. By 1858 Walter's workers had put a much larger, fireproof dome in place. It was made of 8,909,200 pounds (4,041,000 kilograms) of cast iron. They were aided by a new machine called the steam-powered *crane.*

The new Capitol dome under construction in the 1860s. ▶

Other, smaller changes were to come after the Civil War. The Capitol was *remodeled*. Gas and then electric light were added. Many additions were made to the grounds and the other buildings that make up the Capitol Complex. But by the end of the Civil War, the Capitol was largely the same grand building we know today.

Thousands of red, white, and blue balloons soar about the Capitol as the nation celebrates the two hundredth anniversary of the United States Constitution. ▶

CHAPTER THREE

The Capitol Today

Every year, millions of visitors come to the United States Capitol. They arrive from across the country and from all over the world. They come to see the places where the important decisions guiding America are made.

Visitors can take tours of many parts of the Capitol. Sections that are open to the public include the Old Senate Chamber, the Old Supreme Court Chambers, and the National Statuary Hall, which has statues from almost every state.

Did You Know?

• The Capitol is sometimes called "the temple of liberty." It takes its name from a temple that once stood in ancient Rome.

• By 1827, building the Capitol had cost more than $2 million, a huge sum of money at the time.

◄ *Visitors come from all around, often to learn how America's system of government works.*

The rooms and *corridors* of the Capitol are filled with great works of art and many historical *artifacts*. One of the most impressive is a huge 360-degree painting in the Rotunda. Made by the Italian-born artist Constantino Brumidi, it shows the history of America. Another Brumidi painting covers the Rotunda's ceiling. It shows George Washington being carried up to heaven.

The Capitol is just one part of a larger area known as the Capitol Complex. The complex includes offices for lawmakers and the people who work for them. The complex is also home to the Supreme Court Building and the Library of Congress. In all, the grounds total 274 acres (111 hectares). The complex has grown so large, in fact, that it has its own subway system.

The mural on the ceiling of the Rotunda, painted by Constantino Brumidi. Can you find the image of George Washington? ▶

The Capitol grounds have many *attractions*. They include the United States Botanic Garden, the Taft Memorial and Carillon, and the Bartholdi Fountain, which was designed by the creator of the Statue of Liberty.

There are many places to visit at the Capitol Complex. But perhaps the most important thing to see there is not a building or a painting or a room. What many visitors really come to see at the Capitol is their system of government at work.

◄ *The United States Botanic Garden is home to more than four thousand different types of plants.*

When Congress is *in session*, citizens can watch and listen as their elected representatives discuss new laws. They can also look on from the visitors' galleries of the Senate and the House of Representatives as the laws are voted on.

At the United States Capitol, the American people can witness their government at work. This is what makes the United States the great democracy it is. It also makes the Capitol one of the most enduring symbols of America.

A grand fireworks display lights up the sky over the nation's capital. ▶

Glossary

amateur—A person who does something for fun, not as a job.

artifact—An object made in the past.

attraction—A place or event that people come to see.

barracks—A building that soldiers live in.

capital—A city that is the official home of a state or country's government.

Capitol—The building where the United States Congress meets.

centerpiece—The main or most important part of something.

Congress—The part of the United States government, including the Senate and the House of Representatives, that makes new laws.

cornerstone—The first part of a building that is put into place.

corridor—A hallway.

crane—A machine for lifting and moving heavy objects.

democracy—Government based on the will of the people or their elected representatives.

federal government—The government of the entire United States.

House of Representatives—The lower chamber of the United States Congress.

in session—Meeting.

legislative branch—The part of a government that makes laws.

occupy—To take control of a place.

remodel—To improve or change a building.

representative—An elected official chosen to speak or act for a group of people.

Senate—The upper chamber of the United States Congress.

symbolize—To stand for or represent.

Find Out More

Books

Britton, Tamara L. *The Capitol*. Minneapolis: Checkerboard, 2002.

Giddens-White, Bryon. *Congress and the Legislative Branch*. Chicago: Heinemann, 2005.

Hauck, Eldon. *American Capitols: An Encyclopedia of the State, National and Territorial Capital Edifices of the United States*. Jefferson, NC: McFarland & Company, 1991.

LeVert, Suzanne. *Congress*. Danbury, CT: Franklin Watts, 2005.

Mitchell, Alexander D. *Washington Then and Now*. San Diego: Thunder Bay Press, 2000.

Santella, Andrew. *The Capitol*. Danbury, CT: Children's Press, 1996.

Web Sites

Architect of the Capitol

http://www.aoc.gov/

United States Capitol Historical Society—History & Exhibits

http://www.uschs.org/04_history/04.html

United States Capitol Virtual Tour (Senate)

http://www.senate.gov/vtour/

United States Capitol Virtual Tour (House)

http://clerk.house.gov/histHigh/Virtual_Tours/

Index